Early
SCIENCE
Encyclopedias

PHYSICAL SCIENCE

by Christina Dendy

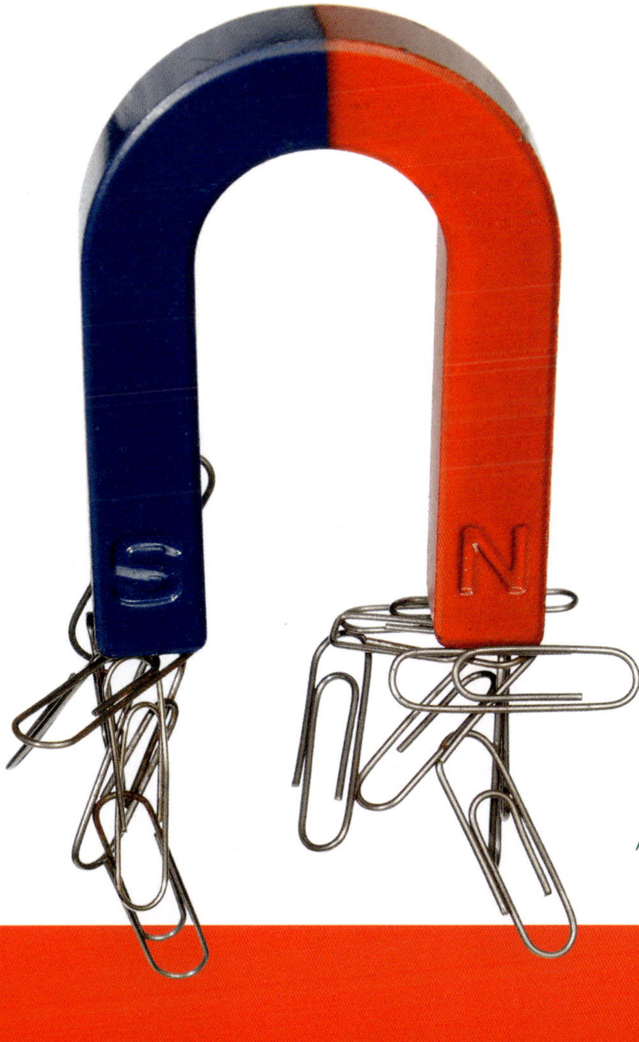

Early Encyclopedias

An Imprint of Abdo Reference
abdobooks.com

abdobooks.com

Published by Abdo Reference, a division of ABDO, PO Box 398166, Minneapolis, Minnesota 55439.

Printed in China.
052024
092024

THIS BOOK CONTAINS RECYCLED MATERIALS

Editor: Marie Pearson
Series Designers: Candice Keimig, Joshua Olson
Production Designer: Joshua Olson

Library of Congress Control Number: 2023949531

Publisher's Cataloging-in-Publication Data

Names: Dendy, Christina, author.
Title: Physical science / by Christina Dendy
Description: Minneapolis, Minnesota: Abdo Reference, 2025 | Series: Early science encyclopedias | Includes online resources and index.
Identifiers: ISBN 9781098294267 (lib. bdg.) | ISBN 9798384913535 (ebook)
Subjects: LCSH: Physical sciences--Juvenile literature. | Technology--Juvenile literature. | Physics--Juvenile literature. | Time and space--Juvenile literature. | Science--Juvenile literature. | Force and energy--Juvenile literature. | Encyclopedias and dictionaries--Juvenile literature.
Classification: DDC 551--dc23

CONTENTS

Living things grow by taking in nonliving things.

Not Alive

Physical science is the study of the nonliving world. Nonliving things include light, air, and electricity. Physical science explores what nonliving things are made of. It looks at how they move and interact. It studies how they affect living things. For example, a tree is alive. It needs nonliving things such as dirt, water, and light.

Understanding the World

Physical science helps people understand the world. Scientists study matter and energy. They learn about motion and forces. They observe sound and light. And they explore electricity and magnetism. Each of these things plays an important role in daily life.

Areas of Physical Science

Chemistry examines what things are made of and how they change. Physics explores how things work. Astronomy focuses on outer space. Geology studies the materials that make up Earth.

Scientists can use tools such as microscopes to study the world.

Universe

The universe is made of everything known to exist. That includes the smallest grain of sand and the largest star. It includes living and nonliving things. Anything people can observe is part of the known universe.

Telescopes allow scientists to study outer space.

A cup of hot liquid loses heat energy as it cools down.

Senses

People use their senses to observe matter and energy. A mug of hot cocoa is made of matter. People feel heat from the cocoa. Heat is a type of energy.

Human Senses

Five main senses help humans observe the world. These are sight, hearing, touch, taste, and smell.

Matter

Matter is anything with volume and mass. Volume is the space that something takes up. A leaf takes up less space than a tree. It has less volume.

Bowling ball

Beach ball

Differences in Mass

These containers have the same volume. But the one on the right has the most matter in the same space. It has more mass than the others.

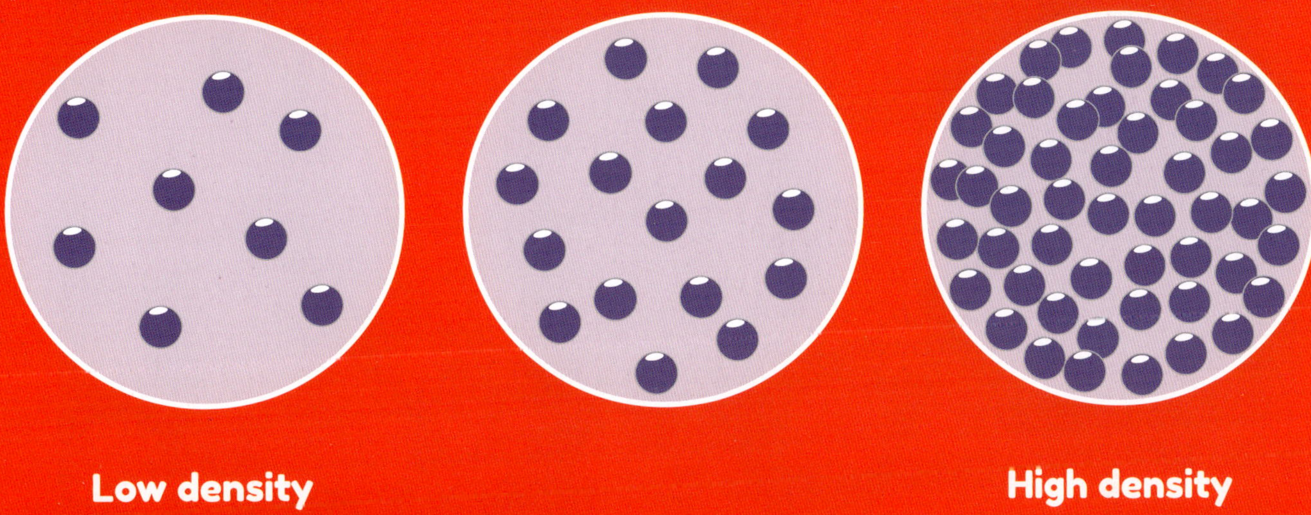

Mass

Mass is the amount of material in something. The more material something has, the more mass it has. A beach ball has more volume than a bowling ball. But it has less mass. More material is packed into the smaller bowling ball.

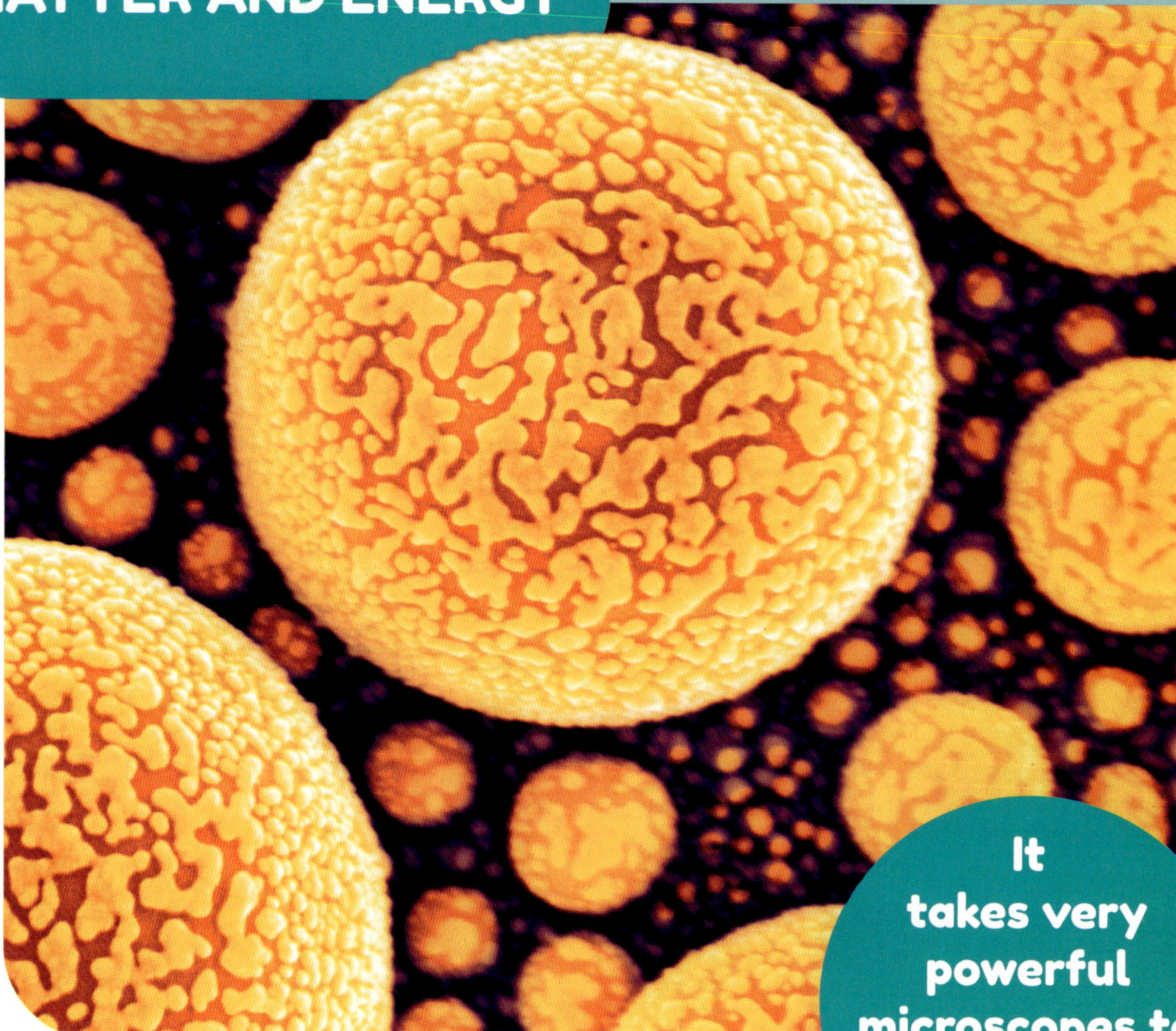

It takes very powerful microscopes to get images of atoms.

Building Blocks of Matter

Matter is made of tiny building blocks called particles. Atoms are one kind of particle. They are too small to see with the human eye.

Molecules

Molecules are also particles. Two or more atoms bond to make a molecule. To bond means to join. A bond between atoms works like glue. It keeps atoms stuck together. A water molecule is made of three atoms. It has two hydrogen atoms and one oxygen atom.

Water Molecule

Each water molecule bonds two hydrogen (H) atoms with one oxygen (O) atom. That's why the symbol for water is H_2O.

Chemicals

Groups of particles combine to form substances. A substance is also called a chemical. Water is a substance. It is made up of many water molecules. A substance can be made from one type of particle. It can also be made from many types of particles.

All matter, including solid objects such as a book, is made of chemicals.

Periodic Table of Elements

The Periodic Table is organized by atomic number.
This is the number of protons in an element.

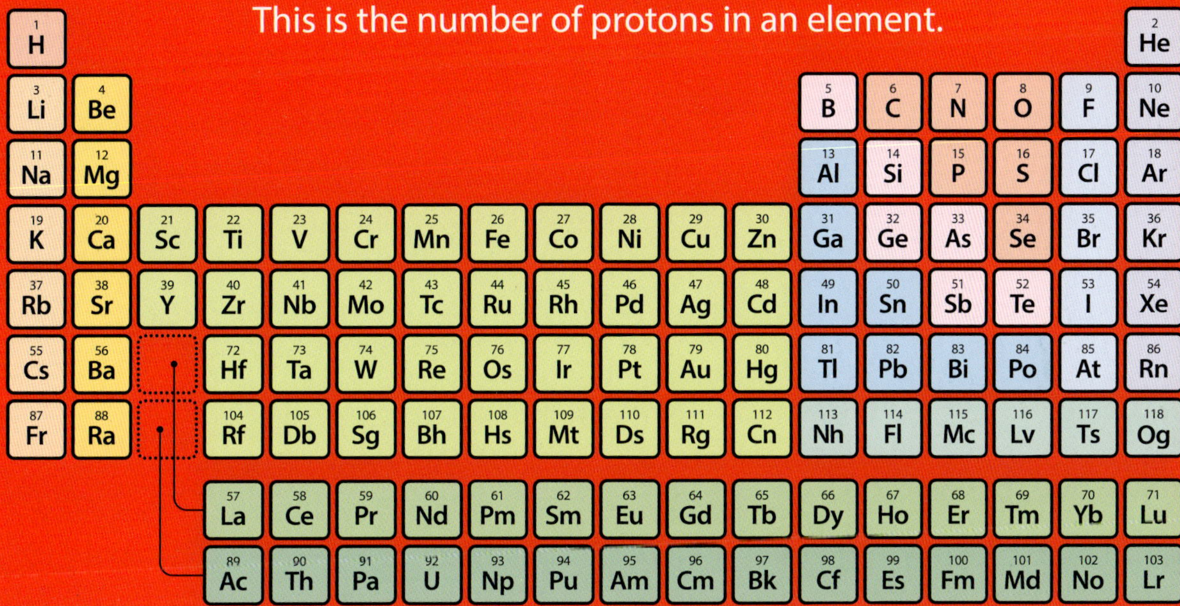

Chemical Elements

A chemical element is the simplest type of substance. It has only one type of atom. It may be made of separate single atoms. Or the atoms may be bonded together as molecules. An element cannot be broken into a simpler substance. Gold is an element. It has only one type of atom. Scientists have put elements into a chart. The chart is called the Periodic Table of Elements.

Chemical Compounds

Some molecules have more than one type of atom. A substance made from this type of molecule is called a chemical compound. All of the molecules in a compound are the same.

Describing Matter

Matter has different properties. A property is how something looks, feels, or acts. Physical properties can be observed. Examples are shape, color, and size.

Foods come in different shapes, colors, and textures.

Physical Properties

Physical properties can change. But the matter's basic makeup stays the same. For example, a piece of paper can be small or large. It can be

Folding paper into different shapes changes its physical properties.

flat or crumpled. It is still paper.

States of Matter

Sometimes matter changes forms. These forms are called states of matter. There are four common states of matter. These are solid, liquid, gas, and plasma.

A glass can hold both a solid, *ice*, and a liquid, *soda*.

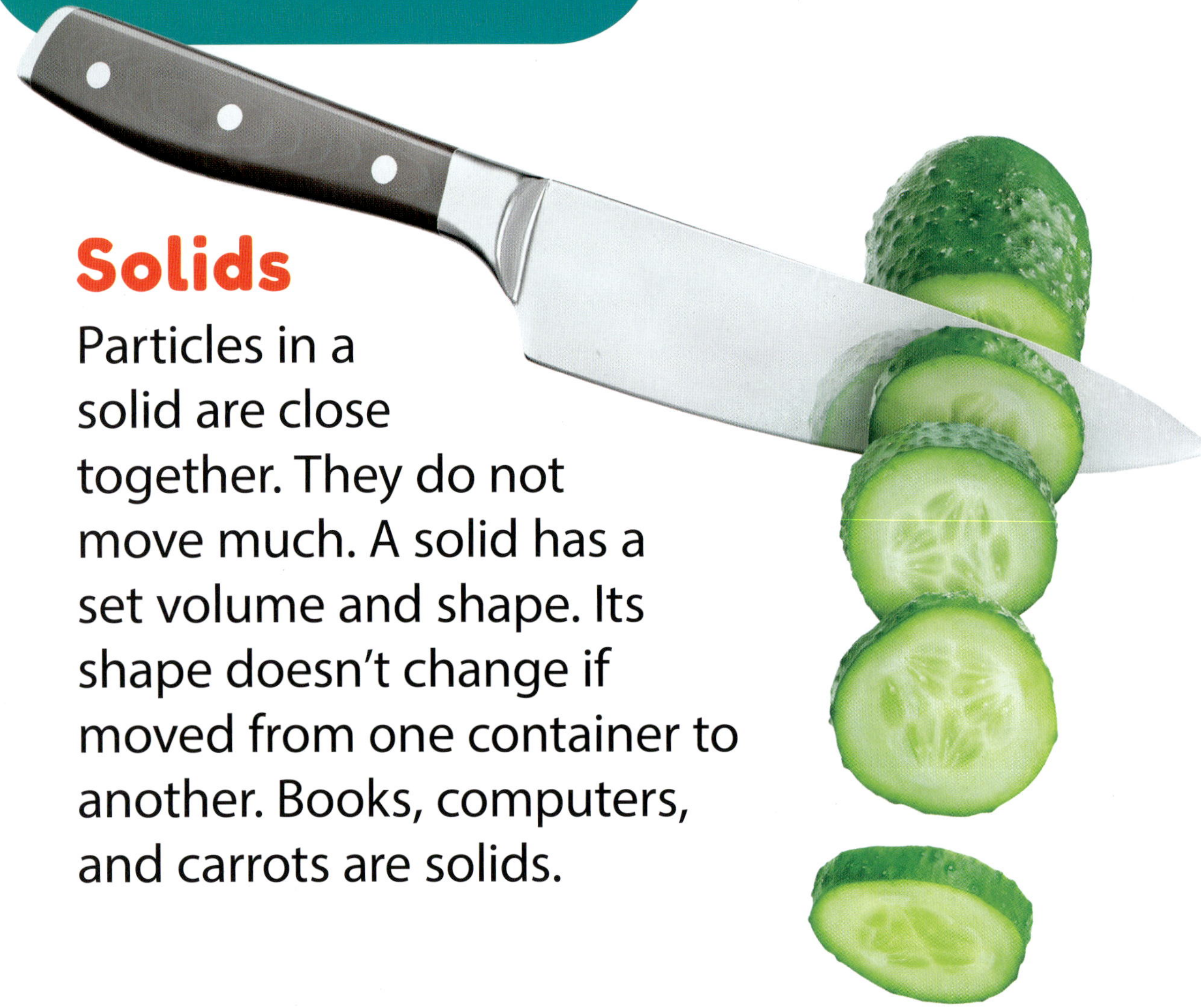

Solids

Particles in a solid are close together. They do not move much. A solid has a set volume and shape. Its shape doesn't change if moved from one container to another. Books, computers, and carrots are solids.

FUN FACT!

Some slime is neither a liquid nor a solid. It can act like both.

Outside forces can change a solid's shape, such as when a knife cuts a cucumber.

Liquids

Particles in a liquid are farther apart than in a solid. They move more freely. A liquid has a set volume. But it does not have a set shape. It takes the shape of the container it is in. Milk and water are liquids.

Because it is a liquid, milk spreads out when spilled.

Gases

A gas does not have a set shape or volume. Particles in a gas can spread out to fill a container. They can be squeezed into smaller spaces. Air is made of many different gases. Air has oxygen. People need oxygen to breathe. It also has carbon dioxide. Plants need this gas.

Balloons can be filled with helium gas, which allows them to float.

Plasma

Plasma is rarely seen on Earth. It can be made by heating gas. Like gas, plasma has no set shape

FUN FACT!

Liquids and gases are both fluids. A fluid is a substance that flows.

Lightning heats the air around it to 50,000 degrees Fahrenheit (27,800°C).

or volume. Particles in plasma also move more freely than in solids and liquids. Lightning and stars are made of plasma.

The Sun provides most of Earth's energy.

Energy

Energy is the ability of matter to do work. It is how matter changes and moves. Turning a page in a book takes energy. So does thinking about what is read. Light that helps a reader see a book is also energy. All work uses some type of energy.

Mechanical Energy

Energy takes many forms. Matter uses mechanical energy to move or stay still. Two types of mechanical energy are kinetic energy and potential energy.

An archer uses energy to pull back an arrow.

Children have potential energy at the top of a slide.

Potential Energy

Matter that is not moving has potential energy. This energy is stored. A cart sitting at the top of a hill has potential energy.

Kinetic Energy

Kinetic energy is the energy of motion. Potential energy becomes kinetic energy when an object moves. As the cart rolls down the hill, its potential energy turns into kinetic energy.

As they go down the slide, children's potential energy becomes kinetic energy.

Other Energy Types

There are many other types of energy. A campfire has light energy and heat energy. The fire crackling is sound energy. Electricity is also energy.

Food has energy that people's bodies can use.

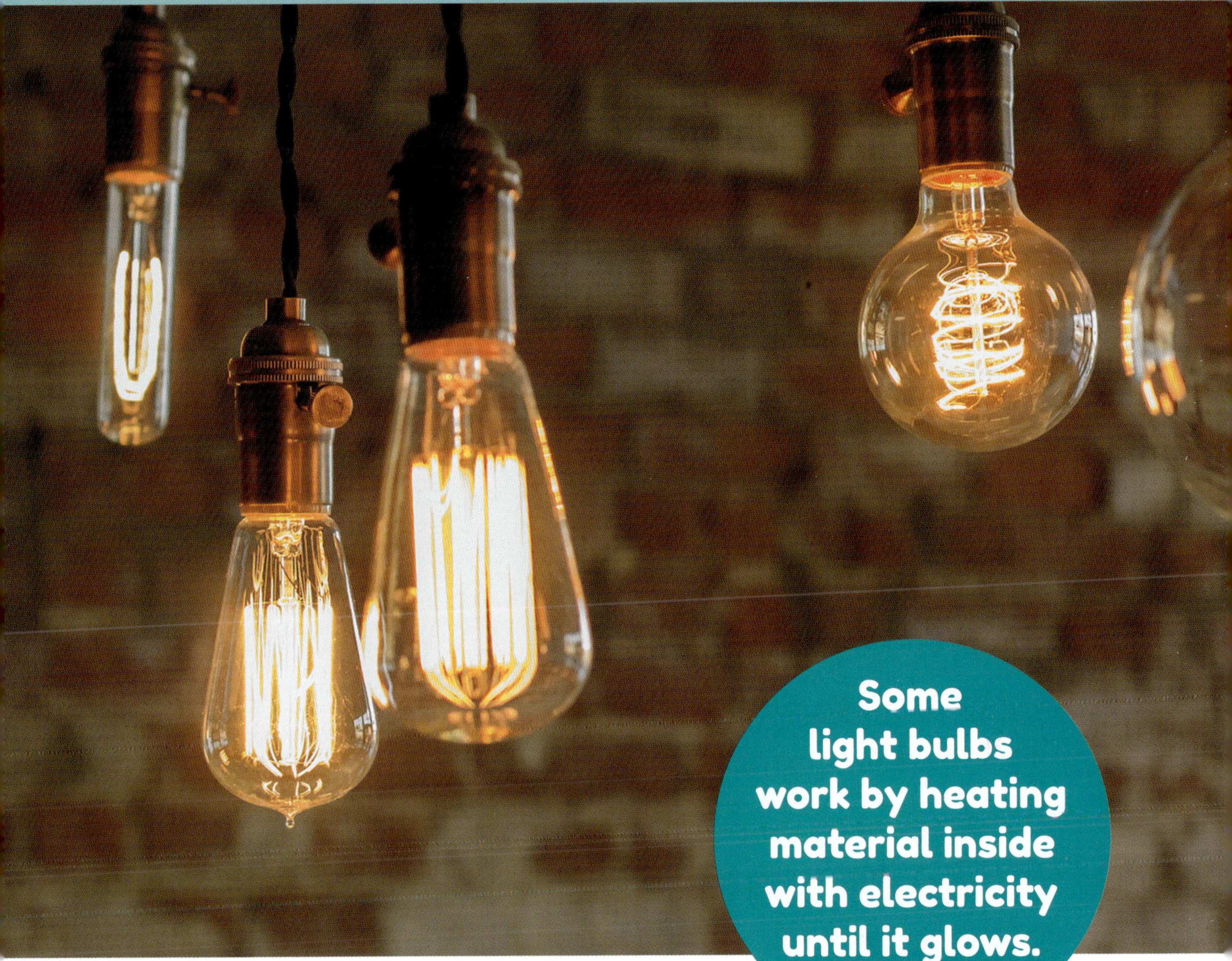

Some light bulbs work by heating material inside with electricity until it glows.

Energy Changes

Energy cannot be created or destroyed. But it does change from one form to another. A light bulb turns electricity into light and heat.

Energy and States of Matter

All matter has energy. Solids have the least energy. Gases and plasmas have the most energy. Adding energy to matter can change it from solid to liquid to gas. Removing energy can change matter from gas to liquid to solid.

Ice cream melts into a liquid as its temperature rises.

Heat Changes

Heat can change a state of matter. The hotter something is, the more energy it has. Its particles move more freely. The colder something is, the less energy it has. Its particles move less.

Refrigerators remove some heat energy from food placed inside them.

Warming Up

When heat rises, solids melt. They turn into liquids. More heat makes liquids evaporate. They turn into gases.

Hot Air Rises

The particles in hot air are more spread out than in cold air. This makes hot air rise above cold air.

People use thermometers to measure temperature.

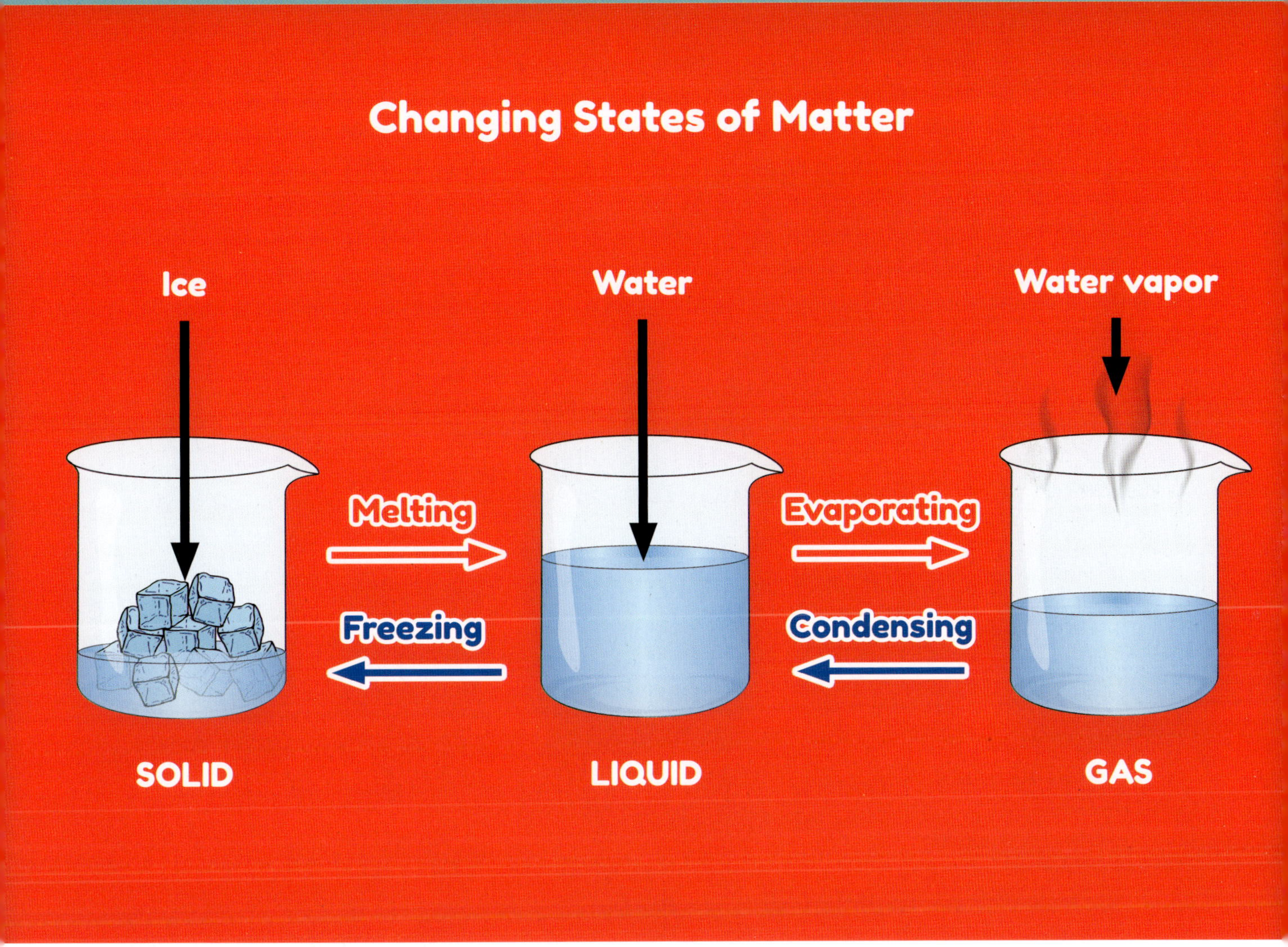

Cooling Down

When heat decreases, gases turn into liquids. This is called condensation. Removing more heat makes liquids turn into solids. This is called freezing.

Matter is always moving at least a little bit. Nothing is absolutely still.

Motion

Motion is a change in something's position. Matter is always moving. A balloon rises. Wind blows. Water flows. People travel.

Describing Motion

Motion is a kind of work. It turns potential energy into kinetic energy. Motion can have speed. Speed is the distance something travels in a certain amount of time.

Speedometers in cars measure speed and help drivers follow speed limits.

Force

Motion happens when forces act on matter. A force is a push or a pull on an object. It changes an object's speed or direction. A person uses force to push a cart. A person uses force to pull a wagon.

A baseball player uses force to throw a baseball.

Two people can work together to move a load. One person pushes, *right*. The other pulls, *left*.

Working Together

More than one force can act on the same object. Two people can work together to move a heavy item. One pushes the object. The other pulls the object. The two forces work together to move the item.

In a game of tug-of-war, two teams use force to pull a rope in opposite directions.

Working against Each Other

Forces can also work against each other. An item's movement depends on the strength of each force. These forces determine the direction and speed of the motion.

Balanced Forces

Balanced forces move in opposite directions. They have equal strength. They cancel each other out. The object does not move.

Unbalanced Forces

Unbalanced forces also move in opposite directions. But they have unequal strength. The object moves in the direction of the stronger force.

A person pushing a shopping cart uses a stronger force than the resistance between the wheels and the floor. The cart moves forward.

Inertia

Moving objects keep moving in the same direction at the same speed. Their motion changes only if an unbalanced force acts on them. Similarly, nonmoving objects do not move. They start moving only when an unbalanced force acts on them. This idea is called the law of inertia.

A soccer ball does not move until an outside force, such as a player's kick, acts on it.

Because ice is smooth, a hockey puck is able to slide for a while before the rubbing of the ice stops it.

Moving a Puck

A hockey puck sits on the ice until a person hits it. The puck keeps moving in one direction until the goalkeeper stops it. Or another player might hit the puck in a different direction.

Momentum

Momentum measures the strength of an object's motion. Objects with more mass have more momentum. A large truck and a small car move at the same speed. The truck has more mass, so it has more momentum. It takes more force to stop or start the large truck.

Equal and Opposite

When objects run into each other, they affect each other. Each object applies force on the other. That force is equal in strength. It is opposite in direction. For example, a child kicks a ball on the ground. The foot applies force in one direction. The ball applies equal force in the opposite direction. The ball has little mass and goes flying. The child has much more mass and stays still. The force from the kick is an action. The force from the ball is a reaction.

A person kicking a ball feels the force of that ball on his or her foot.

Pushing down on a spring produces tension force.

Contact Forces

Many kinds of forces affect matter. Contact forces happen when objects are touching. Kicking, throwing, and twisting are contact forces. Tension is another contact force. It happens by pulling opposite ends of an object such as a rope.

Pressure

Pressure is the amount of force applied to an object. The more force that's applied, the greater the pressure. Pressure can change an object's state of matter.

Friction

Friction is a contact force. It happens when two objects rub against each other. Friction goes against the direction of a motion. It slows movement such as sliding and rolling.

When a car driver hits the brakes, friction between the tires and the road stops the car.

Smooth and Rough

The type of surface affects how strong friction is. Smooth surfaces cause less friction. Objects move more quickly over them. Rough surfaces cause more friction. Objects tend to slow down as they move over rough surfaces.

Ice skates have blades that are thin and smooth in order to reduce friction.

A person must apply more force to move a toy car over carpet than to move it over a hard floor.

Toy Car

A toy car can move faster and farther on a wood floor than on carpet. Friction from rough carpet will slow and stop it. The car needs an outside force to keep it moving.

No-Slip Socks

Socks slip easily on a smooth floor. Some socks have rubber on the bottom to create more friction. This prevents slips and falls.

Boat propellers can spin thousands of times a minute to push the boat forward.

Thrust

Thrust is a contact force. It pushes an object forward. It can come from a propeller pushing gas or liquid behind the object. The spinning blades of a boat's propeller push water behind the boat. This moves the boat forward.

Drag

Drag is a contact force. It goes against the direction of a moving object. It happens when an object moves through a gas or liquid. These materials push against the object. This slows down the object.

When water pushes back against a boat, the boat experiences drag.

Noncontact Forces

Sometimes an object pushes or pulls on another object without touching it. This is called noncontact force. Gravity is a noncontact force. Gravity pulls objects with mass toward each other.

Isaac Newton

Isaac Newton lived from 1643 to 1727. He studied physics. He came up with ideas about motion, inertia, and momentum. He first described gravity as a force.

People fall back to the ground after jumping because of gravity.

Albert Einstein studied light and energy in addition to gravity.

Explaining Gravity

Scientists do not know exactly how gravity works. In the early 1900s, a scientist named Albert Einstein came up with an idea about gravity. He said that gravity happens when matter bends the space around it.

All objects exert gravity on all other objects, but the gravity of small objects is very weak.

Mass and Gravity

The more mass an object has, the stronger its gravity is. A huge object such as Earth has a lot of mass. Its strong gravity keeps things on the planet's surface. Gravity also keeps the Moon circling around Earth.

Weight

Weight is affected by mass and gravity. It is the force of gravity one object applies on another. The stronger the gravity, the more weight an object has. And the more mass, the greater the object's weight. On Earth, an object's weight is the force of Earth's gravity on it.

The Moon and Earth both bend space. Because the Moon has less mass, it gets stuck following a curved path around Earth. That path is called an orbit.

It takes a lot of fuel to launch a spacecraft into space.

Leaving Gravity

Objects on Earth have much less mass than Earth. They need another force to escape Earth's gravity. Thrust helps airplanes and rockets lift off from Earth's surface.

Bouncing on the Moon

The Moon has less gravity than Earth. Objects weigh less on the Moon than they do on Earth. People can jump higher and bounce farther on the Moon.

Airplane Forces

Many forces act on an airplane when it flies. The thrust and lift must be stronger than the drag and gravity to keep the plane in the air.

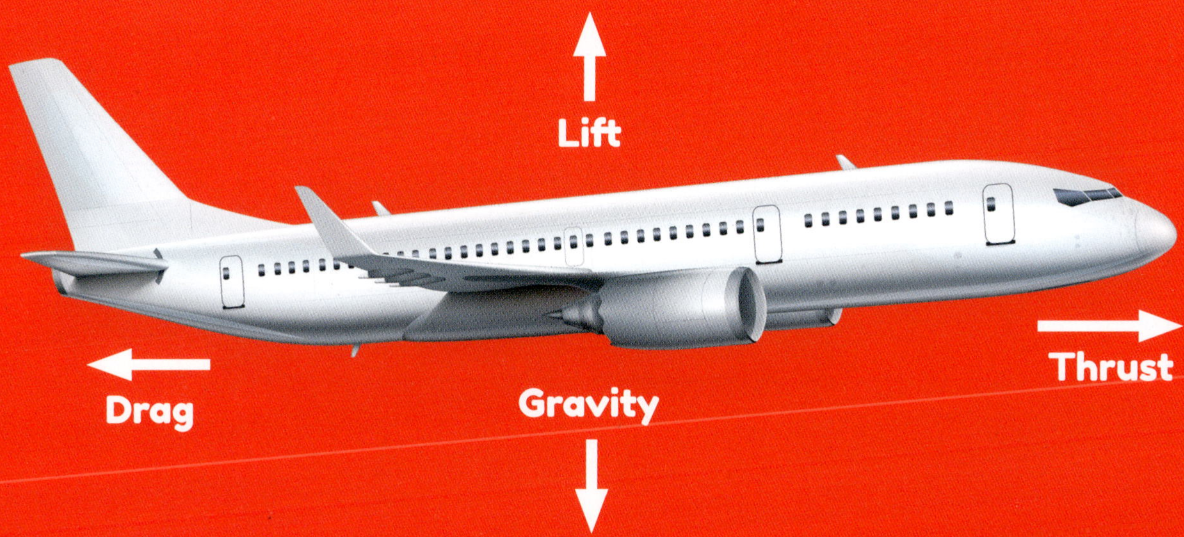

Lift

After thrust pushes objects into the air, lift helps them stay in the air. Lift is a contact force. When objects with certain shapes move through the air, their surfaces turn the flow of air downward. This causes an opposite force that pushes the object upward. Lift also works in water.

Hearing

Hearing is the ability to sense sound. Sound is a kind of energy. When matter vibrates, it makes sound. Musical instruments vibrate. The surface of a drum vibrates when hit. Strings on a guitar vibrate when plucked or strummed.

Parts inside ears allow people to hear sound.

Some jet planes can travel faster in air than the speed of sound.

Sound Waves

Sound energy must travel through a substance. This energy travels as sound waves. The particles in solids are packed close together. Sound waves move quickly from particle to particle. Sound travels more slowly through liquids such as water. Sound moves most slowly through gases such as air.

Vocal Cords

People talk by vibrating vocal cords. Vocal cords are flaps or bands inside the throat. They vibrate when air moves over them.

Speakers work by vibrating to produce sound waves in the air.

Sensing Sound

Sound waves themselves cannot be seen. But the vibrations that make sound can sometimes be seen or felt.

Vacuum

A vacuum is the absence of any matter. Sound cannot travel through a vacuum. Much of outer space is a vacuum. It is quiet.

Moving and Changing

Sound waves move away from the object that makes them. People hear sound when the waves reach their ears. Sound waves get weaker as they travel. This makes sound harder to hear over distances.

Hearing Sound

When sound waves enter the ear, the ear sends signals to the brain. The brain then interprets, or makes sense of, the sound waves.

Pitch

Pitch is how high or low a sound is. The faster the vibration of an object, the higher the pitch of the sound. A whistle vibrates quickly. It has a high pitch. A tuba vibrates slowly. It has a low pitch.

When a person blows into a whistle, the air escapes through another hole, creating a sound.

Pitch and Frequency

High pitches with faster vibrations have shorter wavelengths. Low pitches with slower vibrations have longer wavelengths.

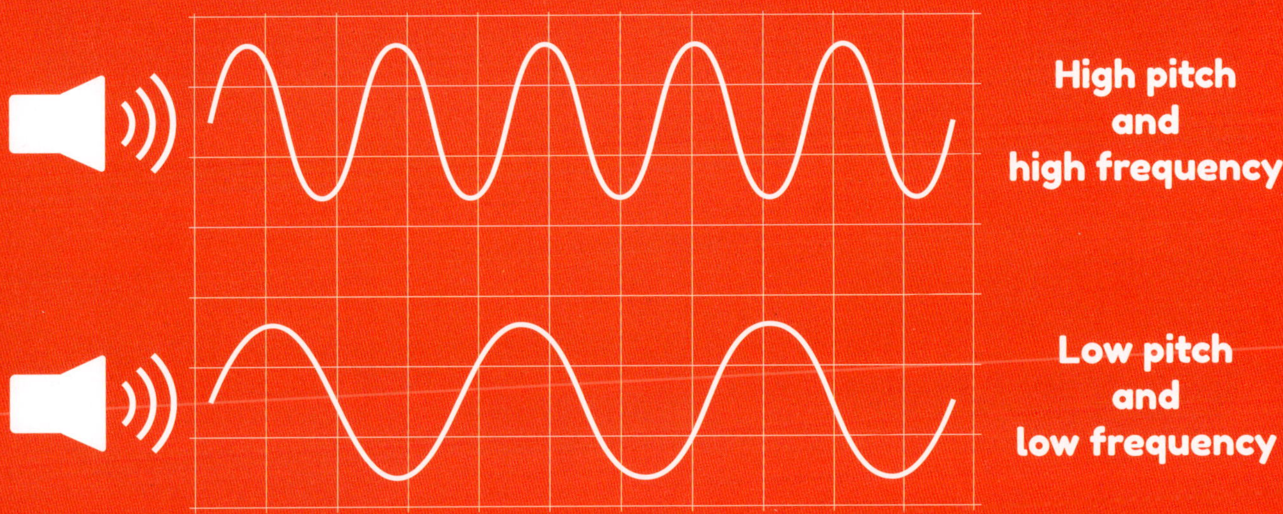

Frequency

Frequency is the number of vibrations in a certain amount of time. Higher pitches have more vibrations per second. They have higher frequencies. Lower pitches have lower frequencies.

Humpback whales communicate underwater by making loud sounds.

Hertz

The frequency of sound is measured in a unit called hertz. One hertz equals one cycle per second. Most people can hear sounds ranging from as low as 20 hertz to as high as 20,000 hertz. Some animals, such as whales and alligators, make sounds too low for people to hear. Other animals, such as dogs and bats, can hear higher sounds than people can.

Volume

Volume is how loud or quiet a sound is. Louder sounds have taller sound waves. Softer sounds have shorter waves.

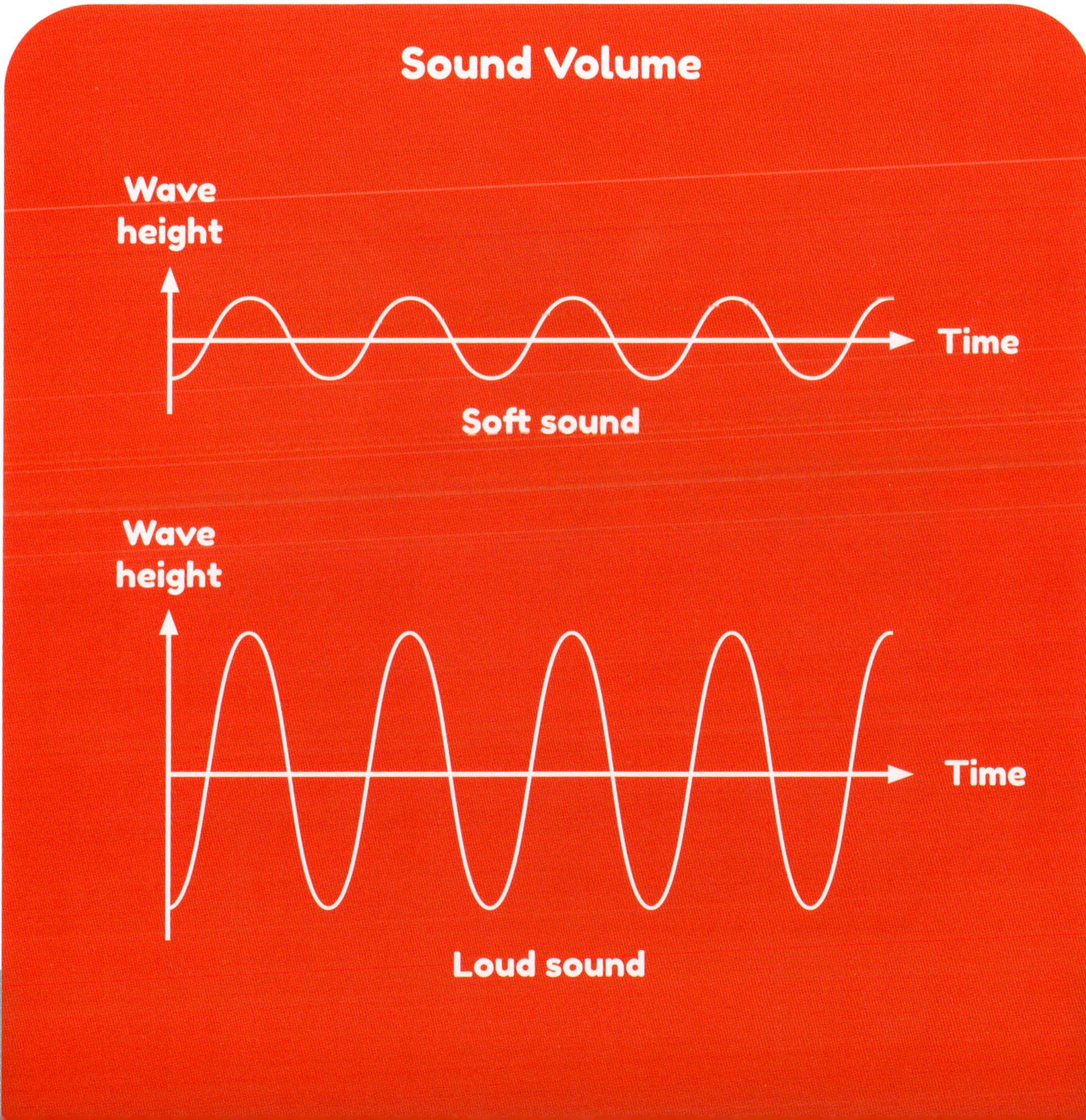

Too Loud

The volume of sound is measured in decibels. A whisper is about 30 decibels. An alarm clock is about 80 decibels. Fireworks reach 140 decibels. Sounds over 85 decibels can hurt a person's hearing.

People put earplugs in their ears to protect their hearing.

Concert halls are designed to take advantage of how sound reflects against objects in a room.

Reflection

The type of matter that sound waves encounter affects sound. When sound waves hit hard surfaces, much of their energy bounces off the surface. This is called reflection.

Echoes happen best with hard surfaces.

Echo

An echo comes from reflection. A person shouts across a canyon. The sound hits a canyon wall. It bounces back to the person. The person hears an echo of the shout.

Absorption

When sound waves hit soft surfaces, much of their energy enters the surface. It does not bounce back. This is called absorption. Less sound is heard. A rock hitting grassy turf makes less sound than a rock hitting a sidewalk. The soft turf absorbs more sound.

FUN FACT!

Snow on the ground absorbs sound. A snowy day outside often sounds quiet.

Bats use the reflection of sound to hunt. This is called echolocation.

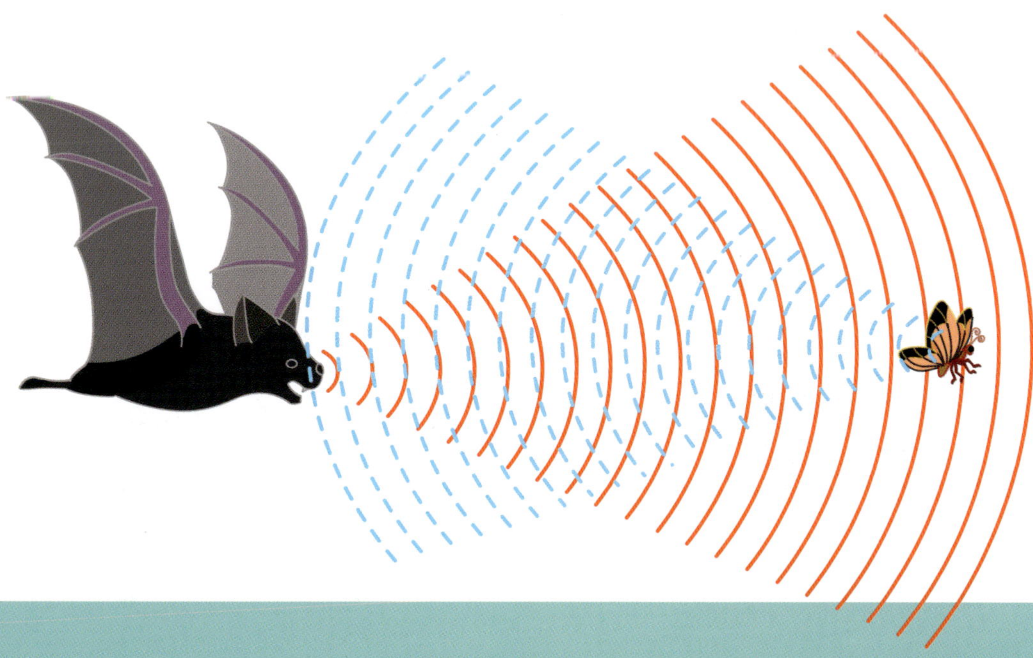

Light from the Sun lets people see during the day.

Light Energy

Light is made of electric energy and magnetic energy. It is a kind of electromagnetic radiation. Radiation is energy that travels as waves or particles. Light lets people see.

Light Waves

People see light when it shines on matter. Like sound, light travels in waves. The waves move in a straight line until they hit a surface. Frequency measures how many light waves pass through a point in a second. Shorter light waves have higher frequencies.

People have invented technology that makes light, such as light bulbs.

Visible Light

People can see some types of light. This is called visible light. Other types of light have wavelengths that are too long or short for people to see.

People can use lamps to make light so they can see at night.

Rainbows happen in the sky when sunlight hits water droplets in the air.

Colors

Visible light is seen as the colors of the rainbow. These colors are red, orange, yellow, green, blue, indigo, and violet. These colors are found in a specific range of wavelengths. Red light has the longest wavelength. Violet light has the shortest. When all the visible wavelengths shine together, they look white.

Windows are transparent. Light shines through them.

Transparent Materials

Light can pass through some materials. These materials are called transparent. Air, water, and glass are transparent. Translucent materials let only some light pass through. Tissue paper is translucent.

Opaque Materials

FUN FACT!

Unlike sound waves, light waves can travel through a vacuum.

Light cannot pass through opaque materials. Many types of metal, wood, and stone are opaque. Light waves bounce off opaque objects. They can create reflections. Mirrors layer glass on a metal such as silver or aluminum. Light waves pass through the glass but reflect off the metal. This creates reflections on the surface of the mirror.

The metal used in mirrors is opaque.

Changing Direction

Light waves can change direction as they pass through some matter. When light passes through a prism, it bends in different directions. That bending separates the light beam into different wavelengths. People see each color of the rainbow.

The Color of the Sky

Air molecules scatter short blue and violet wavelengths more than they scatter long wavelengths. These shorter wavelengths of light make the sky look blue.

Light bends and splits as it passes through a prism. It makes a rainbow.

Night vision imaging devices can use colors such as red and orange for the hottest parts. Colors such as blue and green are for the coolest parts.

Invisible Light

The human eye cannot see many types of light. Heat makes infrared light. This has longer wavelengths than people can see. Some night vision goggles turn infrared light into visible colors. They let people see heat. People use these goggles to see in dark places.

Microwaves

Microwaves are a form of radiation with long wavelengths. Microwave ovens use microwaves to heat food. Food vibrates when it absorbs these waves. That vibration turns into heat. The food warms quickly.

When food vibrates in a microwave oven, molecules rub against each other. The friction from the rubbing produces heat.

Radio Waves

Radio waves have the longest wavelengths. It takes longer for air particles to absorb long light waves. So radio waves travel farther than shorter light waves. This makes radio waves good for sending information across distances. Radios and televisions receive radio waves. They turn the waves into sounds and images.

Ultraviolet Light

The Sun makes many types of light. One is ultraviolet light. This light has shorter wavelengths than people can see. Some ultraviolet light strengthens muscles and bones. Too much can hurt a person's eyes and skin. Ultraviolet light can also kill germs.

People can wear sunglasses to protect their eyes from ultraviolet light.

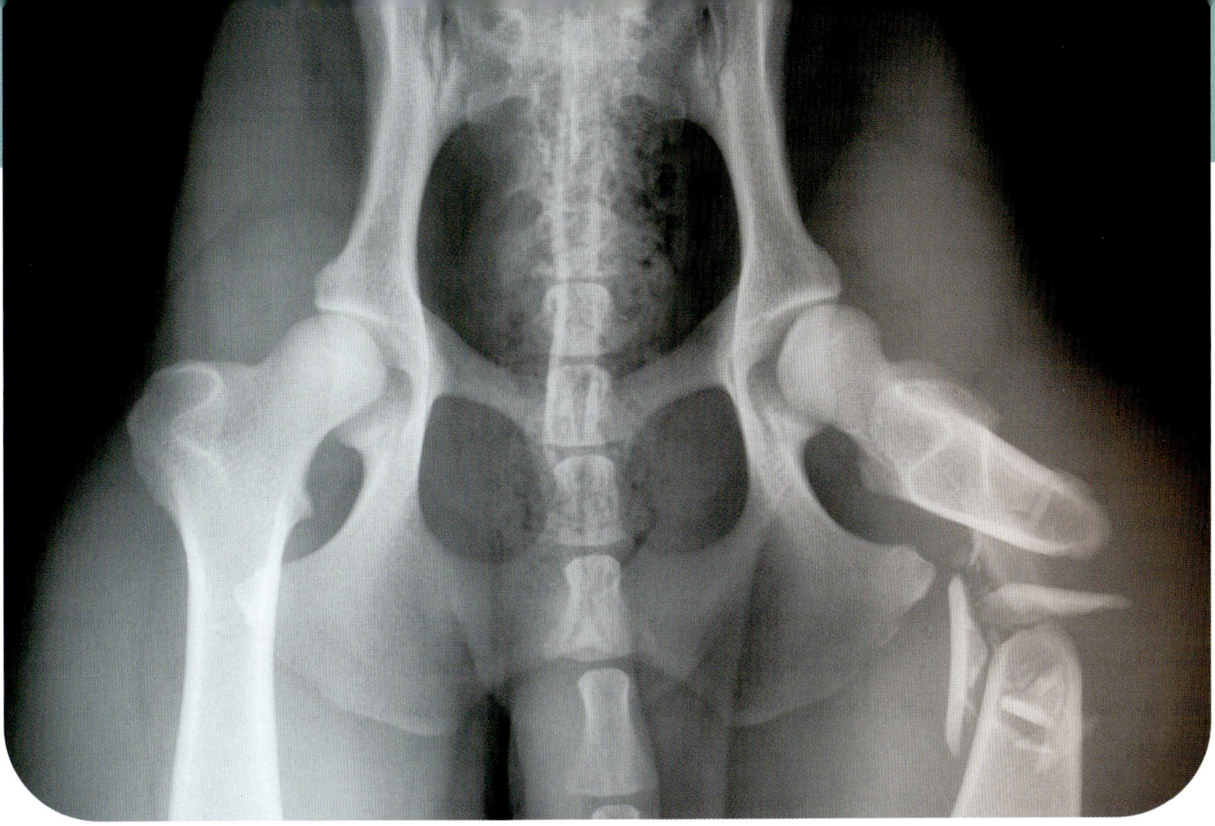

Veterinarians can take X-rays of animals such as dogs to find broken bones.

X-Rays

X-rays have even shorter wavelengths. These high-energy light waves can pass through soft body tissues, such as skin. Doctors use X-rays to take pictures of hard tissues inside bodies. These pictures can show if bones are broken.

FUN FACT!

Bees can see ultraviolet light. So can some birds, reptiles, and other animals.

The *Psyche* spacecraft was launched in 2023 to study an asteroid with the same name. The spacecraft included gamma ray sensors.

Gamma Rays

Gamma rays have the shortest wavelengths. They travel faster than other types of radiation. They can be used to destroy cancer cells.

Dangerous Energy

Too much high-energy radiation can harm living cells. People wear sunblock to protect against ultraviolet radiation. They use protective coverings to block X-rays and gamma rays.

Speed of Light

Light waves travel at different speeds through different types of matter. But light always travels through a vacuum at the same speed. This is called the speed of light. It equals 186,282 miles per second (299,792 kms). Light waves are much faster than sound waves. This is why people see lightning before they hear thunder.

Electromagnetic Spectrum

The electromagnetic spectrum shows the different kinds of light organized by their wavelengths.

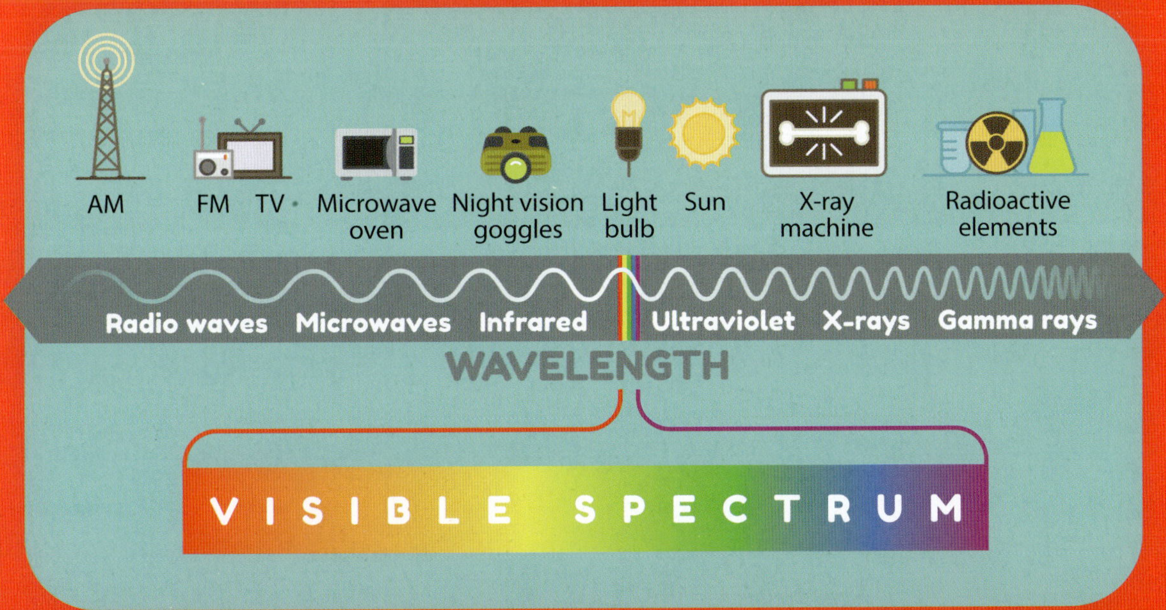

Using Machines

The wagon is an example of a machine. A machine is something that people use to do work. People use many kinds of machines every day.

A wagon uses a simple machine called a wheel and axle.

Moving Sand

Two children want to move a big pile of sand. It would take many trips with a small pail. A bigger pail would take fewer trips. But it would be too heavy to carry. A wagon holds even more sand than a big pail. It also has wheels. This makes it easier to move.

Skate parks are filled with inclined planes.

Simple Machines

The first machines people made were simple machines. Simple machines have a few or no moving parts. They let people use less force to do the same work. This saves people energy.

Inclined Plane

An inclined plane is a simple machine. *Inclined* means "leaning" or "sloping." This machine has a flat surface set at a slope. It helps people move an object between a low and a high place. A ramp is an inclined plane. A person can push or pull something up or down a ramp.

FUN FACT!

A playground slide is an inclined plane.

A person uses a ramp to move a heavy object from a low place to a high place.

Lever

A lever is a simple machine. It is a straight bar or beam that sits on a support. The support is called a fulcrum. A lever uses distance to make work easier. It spreads out the effort across a distance. Effort is the force applied to the lever.

FUN FACT!

A seesaw is a lever.

Using a Lever

A person pushes on one end of the lever. This effort lifts the other end. The end being pushed is farther from the fulcrum than the end being lifted. A long lever lets someone move an object with less force than it would take to move the object directly.

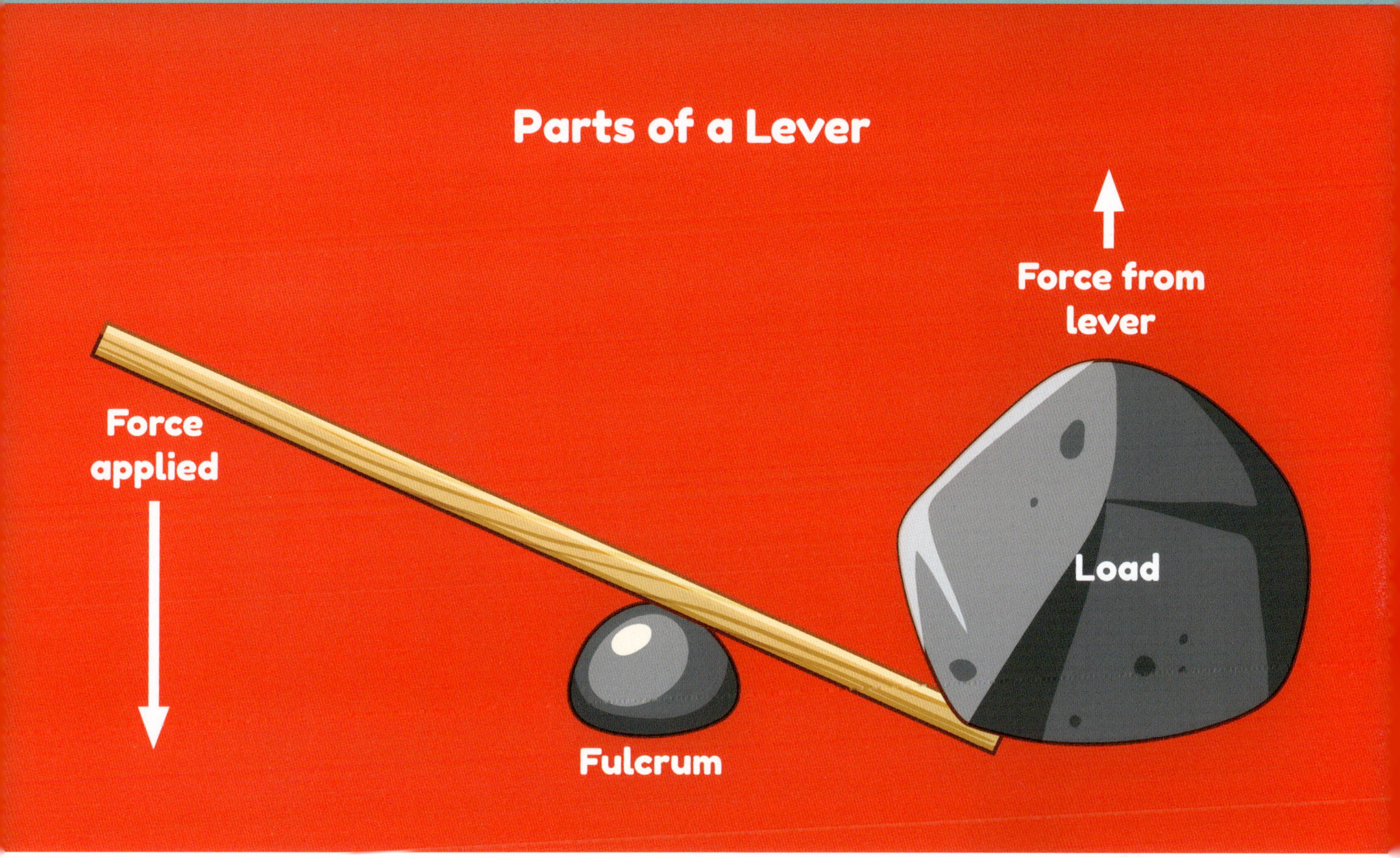

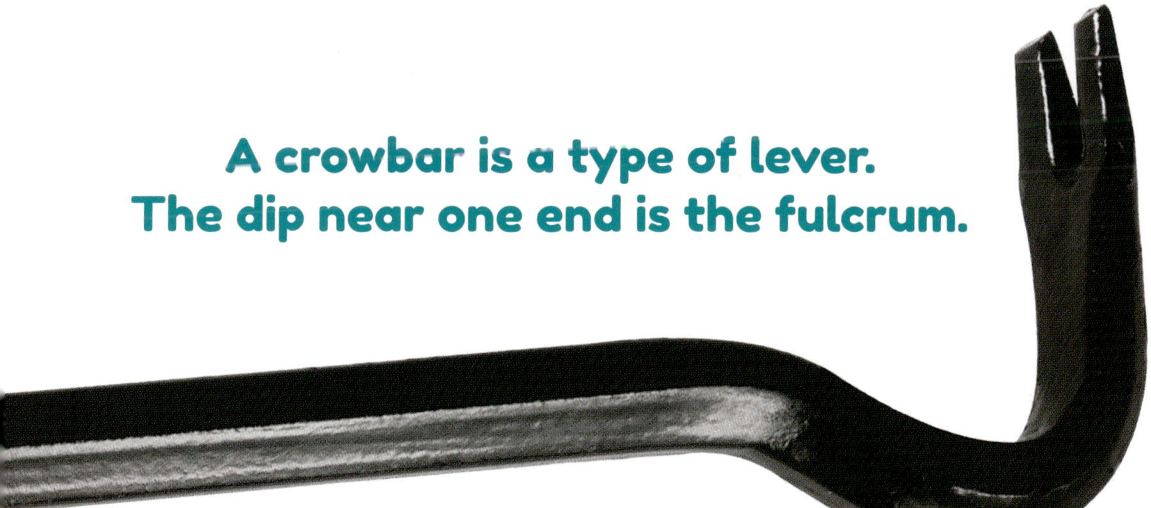

A crowbar is a type of lever. The dip near one end is the fulcrum.

Wheel and Axle

Another simple machine is the wheel and axle. An axle is a rod or bar that fits through the center of a wheel. When force is used, the wheel and axle move together.

A unicycle uses a single wheel and axle.

Using the Wheel and Axle

A wheel and axle can move objects. Wagons, bicycles, and cars all use wheels and axles to move. An object sliding on a flat bottom meets more friction than an object rolling on wheels. Wheels and axles lower friction. They make the work easier.

Force applied to the wheel and axle creates motion.

A pulley raises and lowers a bucket in a well.

Pulley

Pulleys move objects from one point to another. A pulley is a wheel that has a groove cut into it. A rope or cable fits into the groove. Pulling one end of the rope lifts or pulls objects on the other end. People often use pulleys to raise and lower flags.

Wedge

A wedge has a wide end that narrows to a point or edge. Force is applied to the wide end. The force travels to the narrow end. The same amount of force is now in a smaller area. It drives the point or edge into another object. An axe is an example of a wedge.

An axe pushes two halves of a log apart.

Screw

A screw holds objects together. It has a kind of inclined plane called a thread. The thread wraps around an axle.

Using a Screw

A force twists the screw. The thread grips the material of the object. It moves the screw into an object. The screw can be twisted the other way. The thread pushes the screw out of the object.

The thread around a screw is a continual inclined plane.

A drill twisting a screw also applies a pushing force.

Compound Machines

Simple machines can be combined. This makes compound machines. A wheelbarrow combines a lever with a wheel and axle. A pair of scissors combines two levers and two wedges. Compound machines can have many parts. Cars combine many simple machines.

A person's hand provides the energy for scissors to work.

Cranes use pulleys. Engines provide energy for the cranes to work.

Powering Machines

People use energy from their bodies to apply force to some simple machines. Many modern machines use other sources of energy. For example, elevators use pulleys that run on electricity.

Electric Energy

Electricity is electric energy. It can make objects move and work. It is a noncontact force. Every day, people turn on lights. They use smartphones. They watch television. These activities use electricity.

Electricity lets screens light up and show pictures.

Electricity powers lights indoors.

Parts of an Atom

To understand electricity, it is important to understand the parts of atoms. Inside each atom are even smaller particles. These are protons, neutrons, and electrons.

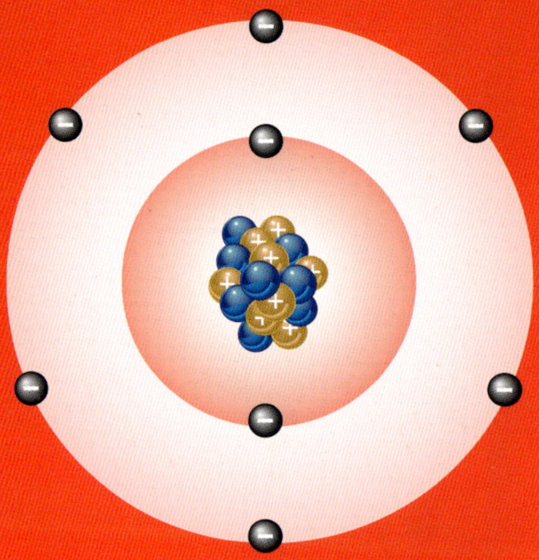

OXYGEN ATOM

- 8 electrons
- 8 protons
- 8 neutrons

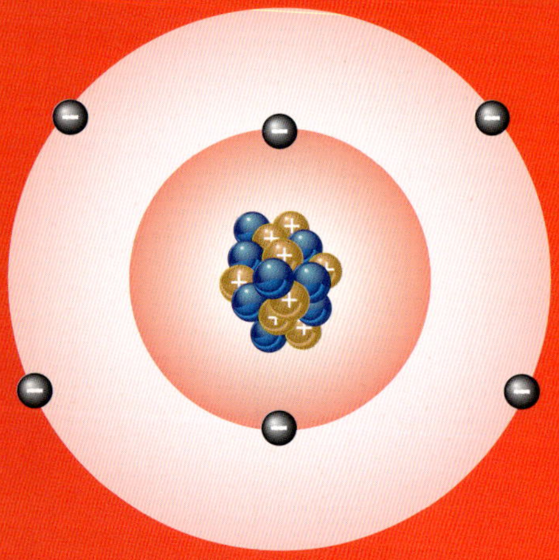

POSITIVE CHARGE

- 6 electrons
- 8 protons
- 8 neutrons

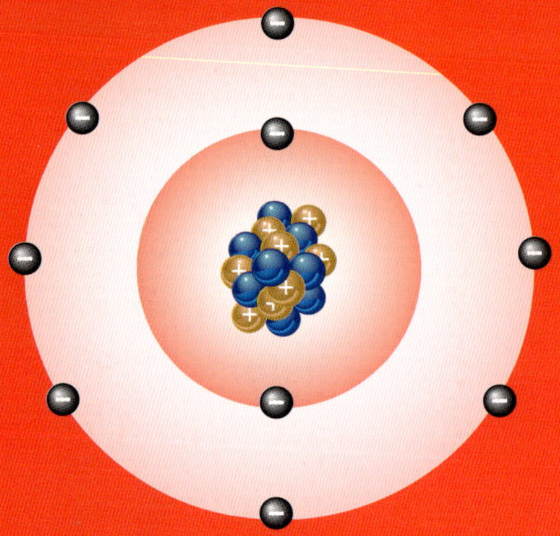

NEGATIVE CHARGE

- 10 electrons
- 8 protons
- 8 neutrons

Charges

Protons have a positive electric charge. Electrons have a negative electric charge. Neutrons have no charge at all.

Positive and Negative

Most atoms have the same number of protons and electrons. The positive and negative charges balance each other. Some atoms lose electrons. They have more protons than electrons. Their charge is unbalanced. These atoms have a positive charge. Other atoms gain more electrons than protons. They have a negative charge. This movement of electrons creates electricity.

FUN FACT!

Clothes tumbling in a dryer rub against each other. They create static electricity.

Forms of Electricity

Electricity can take two forms. These are static electricity and current electricity. Static electricity is the buildup of an electric charge in an object. Rubbing two items together quickly creates friction. This causes electrons to pass from one material to the other. Static electricity is generated.

A Van de Graaff generator rubs rubber bands on felt. This pulls electrons from the felt to a metal ball. When a person touches the ball, his or her hair stands on end.

A balloon rubbed against a person's hair gains electrons. It becomes charged. An invisible electric field forms around the balloon.

Push and Pull

Static electricity creates an electric charge in the space around the items. This is called an electric field. When matter passes through that field, electricity acts on it. The electricity pulls or pushes on the matter. Static electricity can make a person's hair stand on end.

When a plastic comb has run through dry hair, it becomes charged.

Opposites Attract

An object with a positive charge and an object with a negative charge attract each other. To attract means to pull something near. Sometimes the objects stick together.

Repelling Charges

Objects with the same charge repel each other. To repel means to push away. Two balloons with static electricity have the same charge. If the balloons are held close together, they push each other away.

Balloons with different charges stick together.

Balloons with the same charge push away from each other.

Lightning happens when electricity builds up in a cloud. It can jump to another cloud or to the ground.

Moving between Objects

Static electricity can move between objects. This happens when an object with a charge touches an object without a charge. Extra electrons move from the charged to the uncharged object. People feel a shock when static electricity moves between them and something else.

Balancing

Electrons also move when an object with a negative charge touches one with a positive charge. Then extra electrons in the negatively charged object move to the positively charged object. The charges balance each other.

Static electricity jumps between two points on a Wimshurst machine.

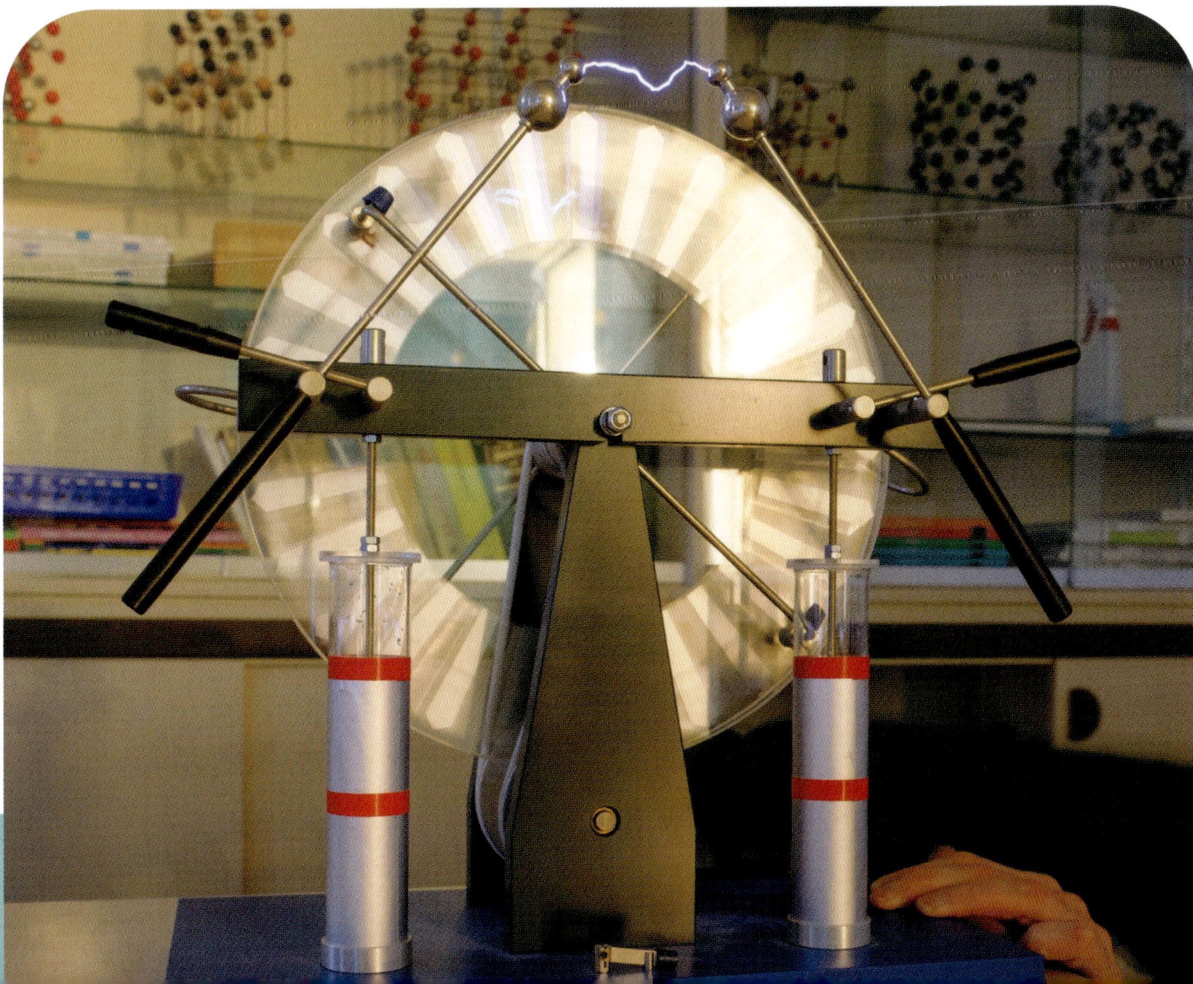

Current Electricity

Some electricity moves along a path. It flows from one object to another. This is current electricity. An electric current can travel through a vacuum. It also travels through matter.

Current electricity moves through a conductor into a car battery.

Conductors and Insulators

Materials that carry electric currents are called conductors. Most metals are conductors. These metals include copper, aluminum, silver, gold, and steel. Materials that do not carry electric currents are called insulators. Glass, plastic, rubber, and dry wood are insulators. Water is an insulator. But it may have substances in it that are conductors, such as salt.

Copper wire for electronics is sold in spools. The wire can be cut to the desired length.

A machine called a Tesla coil can mimic lightning.

Seeing Electricity

Usually people cannot see electricity. But people can see electric currents when they charge particles in the air. Lightning is an example. People may also see static electricity jumping from one object to another. This creates a spark.

Electricity at Work

When a device uses electricity, it turns electric energy into another form of energy. When an electric charge moves, it often makes heat. So electric devices can feel hot.

Computers have fans built into them to help keep them from overheating.

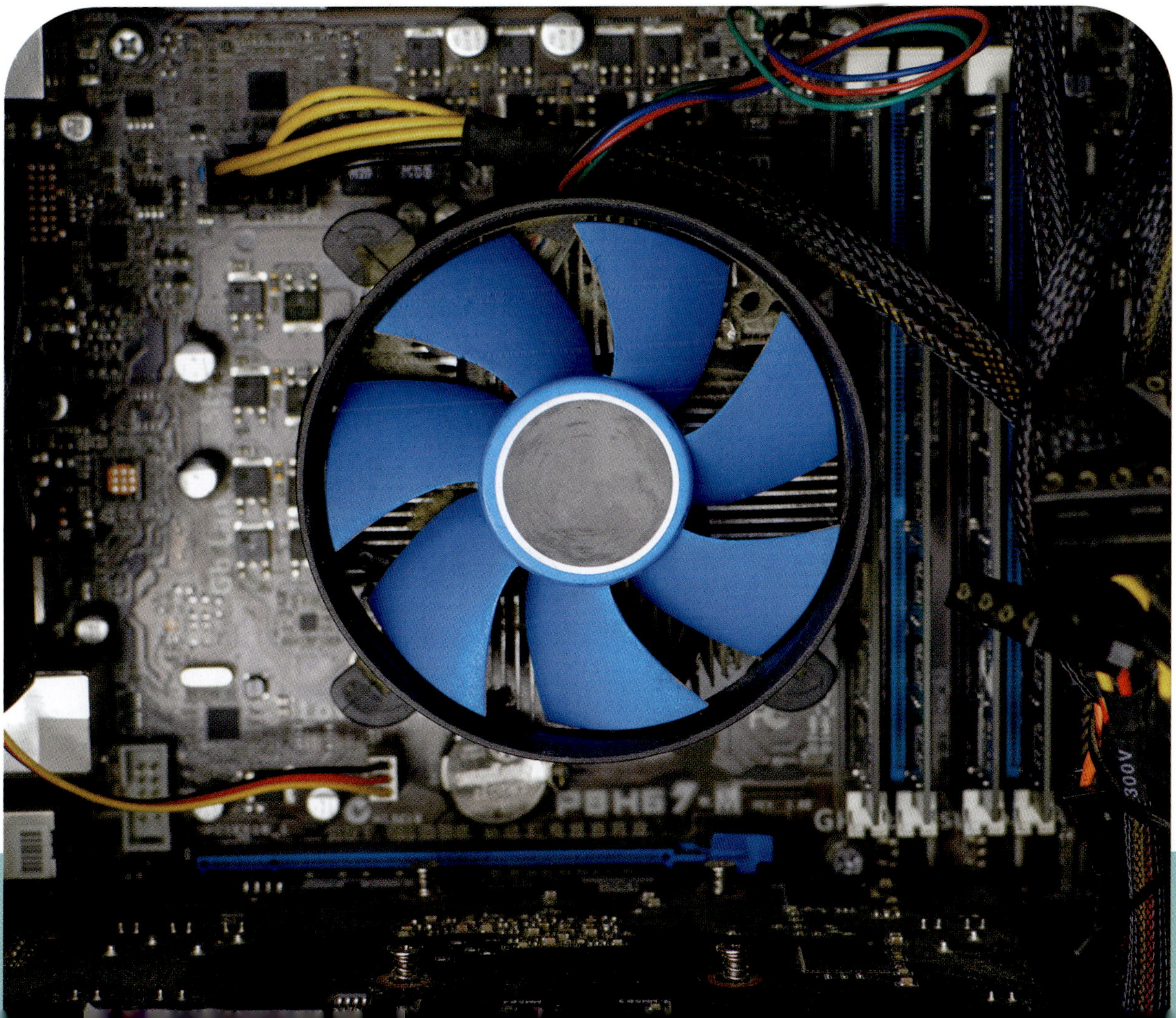

Changing Forms of Energy

Other types of energy can be changed into electricity. Kinetic energy from moving water can be turned into electricity. So can light from the Sun. Burning oil and natural gas releases heat that can generate electricity.

Solar panels turn sunlight into electricity.

Electricity in Life

Electricity is in all matter. The human brain runs on electric energy. An electric eel can give off an electric charge. The electricity shocks other animals. Then the eel can catch them.

Power lines are kept high in the air so people and vehicles can't run into them.

Power Plants

Power plants generate electricity. They have machines that turn other types of energy into electricity. They send electricity along power lines. Power lines carry electricity to homes and businesses. People can plug devices into electric sockets to use this electricity.

Batteries

A battery is another source of electricity. It stores chemical energy. A device is connected to a battery. The battery's chemical energy changes to electricity. The electricity flows into the device.

Batteries come in many shapes and sizes. They can release different levels of electricity.

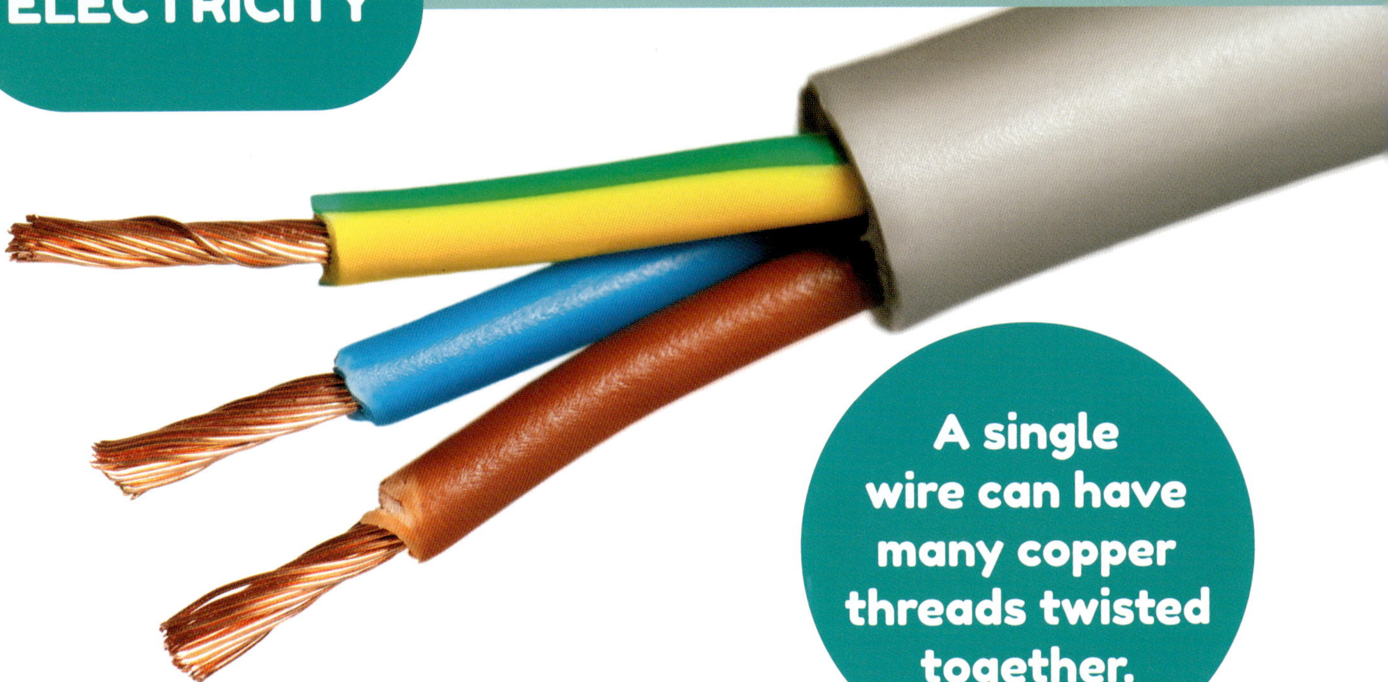

A single wire can have many copper threads twisted together.

Circuits

Electric currents travel on paths called circuits. A circuit connects a source of electric energy to a device that uses electricity. Circuits use wires that conduct electricity. They are wrapped in insulators. This protects people from getting electric shocks.

Switches

Electricity flows along a circuit until something blocks it. A switch is attached to a circuit. A switch can be open or closed. When open, it breaks the circuit's path. This stops the flow of an electric current. When closed, it connects the circuit. This allows electricity to flow.

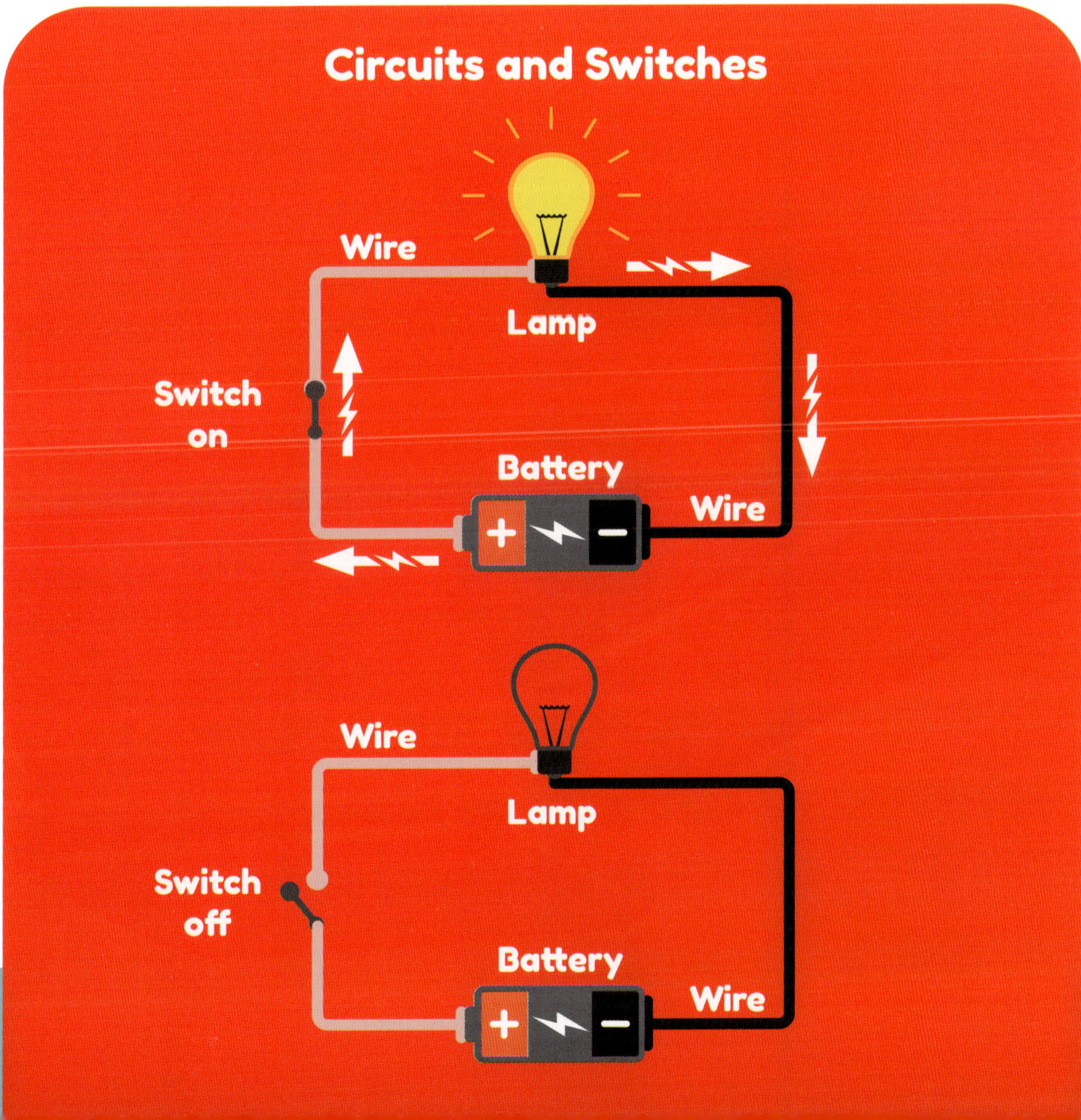

Dangers of Electricity

Human bodies carry small amounts of electricity. A small amount of static electricity gives a mild shock. But too much electricity is dangerous. Power lines and lightning have harmful levels of electricity. They can injure or kill people.

Signs warn people when they are near places with dangerous amounts of electricity.

Electricians often wear rubber gloves to reduce the risk of electrocution.

Staying Safe

Insulation helps protect people. People trained to work with electricity wear protective clothing such as rubber gloves. They turn off the source of electricity before working on equipment.

FUN FACT!

Rubber soles on shoes are insulators.

Letters attached to magnets can be arranged into words.

Sticking Together

A magnet is an object that attracts certain types of metal. Magnets can stick to refrigerator doors. They hold up pictures and papers. Headphones use magnets to make sound. Magnets have many other uses.

Making Magnets

Electrons spin around the center of an atom. Sometimes many electrons spin in the same direction. They make a magnetic field around an object.

FUN FACT!

The hotter a magnet gets, the lower its strength becomes.

Magnetic Field

The magnetic field is shown as curved lines. They are called lines of force. They never cross and are usually invisible.

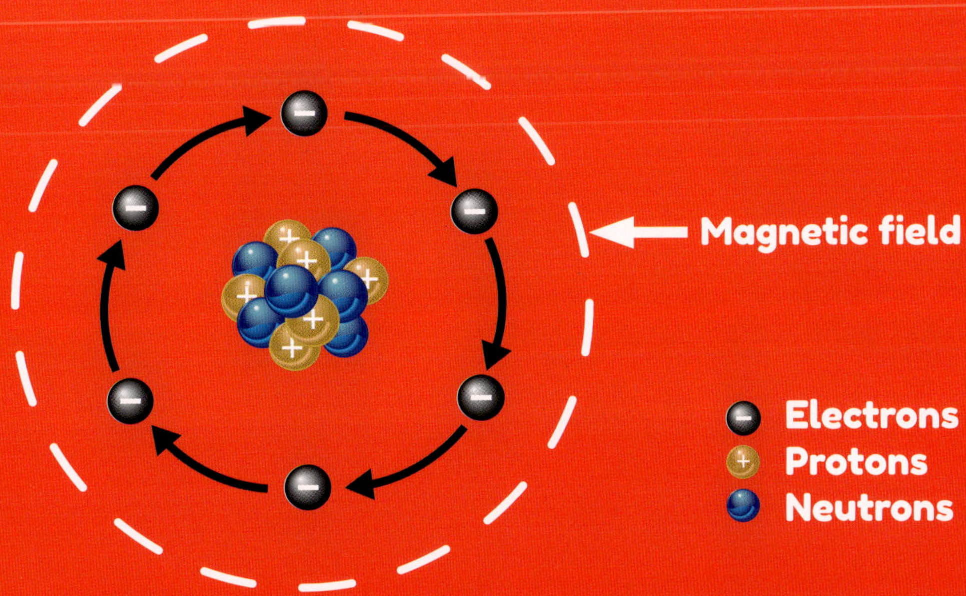

The Magnetic Field

A magnetic field is the area affected by a magnet. Magnetic fields can push or pull objects that pass through them. This force is called magnetism. It is a noncontact force.

FUN FACT!

People can rub a piece of iron in one direction against a magnet for a few minutes. This turns the iron into a magnet.

Toys can use magnets to hold pieces together.

Mining companies can crush mined rock and then use magnets to separate magnetic metals from other materials.

Magnetic Metals

Magnetism attracts certain kinds of metals. Magnetic metals include iron, cobalt, nickel, and some kinds of steel. Some types of rock contain magnetic metals too. Magnetite is a rock with iron.

Gold is a soft metal. It is easily scratched.

Nonmagnetic Metals

Magnets do not attract some other types of materials. Aluminum, brass, copper, gold, lead, silver, and tin are nonmagnetic metals. Nonmetal materials such as wood, paper, plastic, cotton, and wool are not magnetic.

Magnetic Poles

Magnets have positive and negative poles. Poles are opposite ends of something. Magnets have a north pole and a south pole. The magnetic force of a magnet is strongest at each pole.

FUN FACT!

Machines called metal detectors use magnets to find buried metal objects.

Magnets sometimes identify the north pole with an *N* and the south pole with an *S*.

North and South

The opposite poles of magnets attract each other. A north pole and a south pole pull toward each other. The same poles of magnets repel each other. Two north poles push each other away.

Holding the opposite poles of two magnets toward each other pulls them together.

Earth's Magnetic Field

Earth's core is made of iron. It creates a large magnetic field around Earth. This field shields the planet from harmful particles from the Sun.

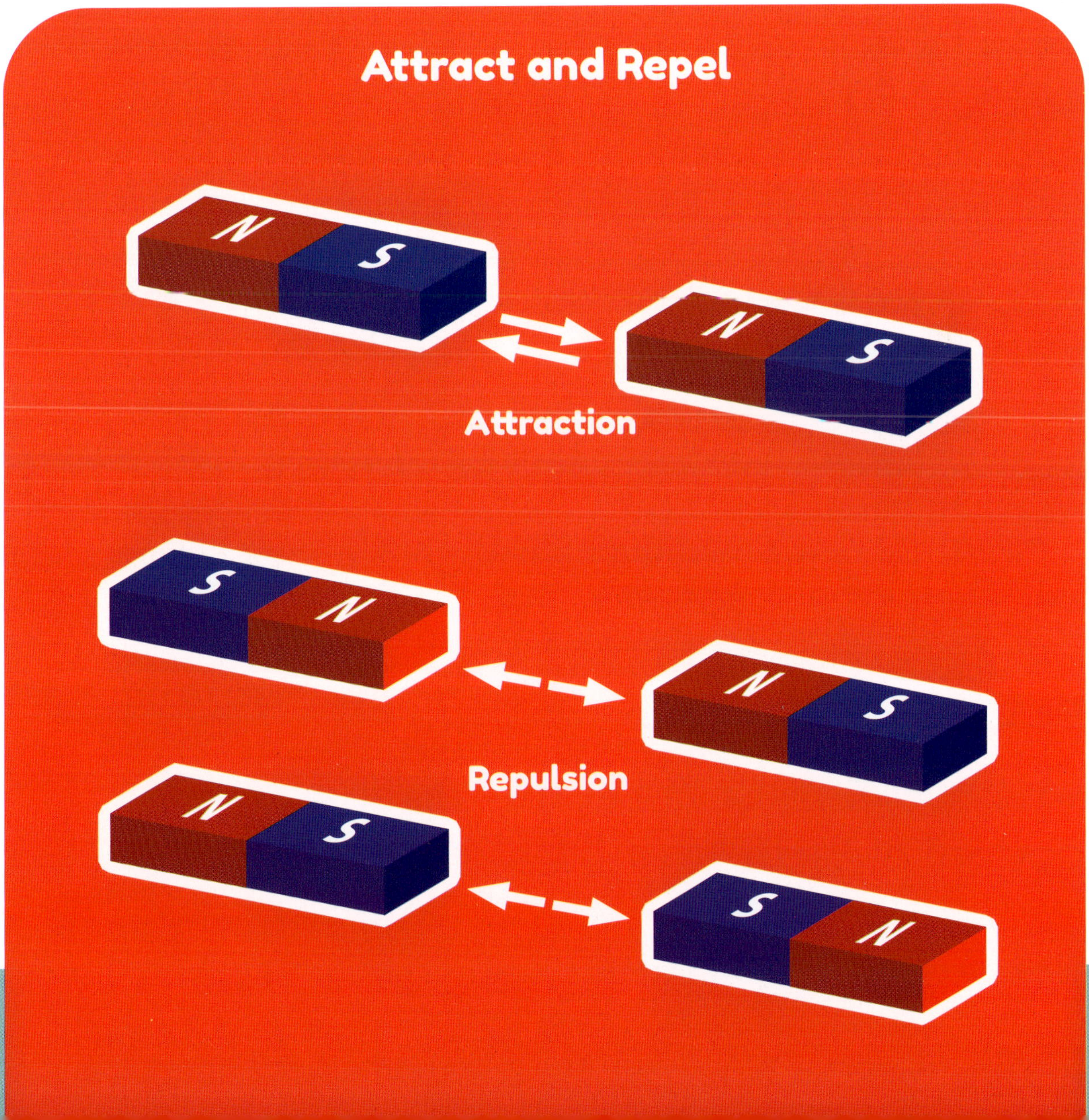

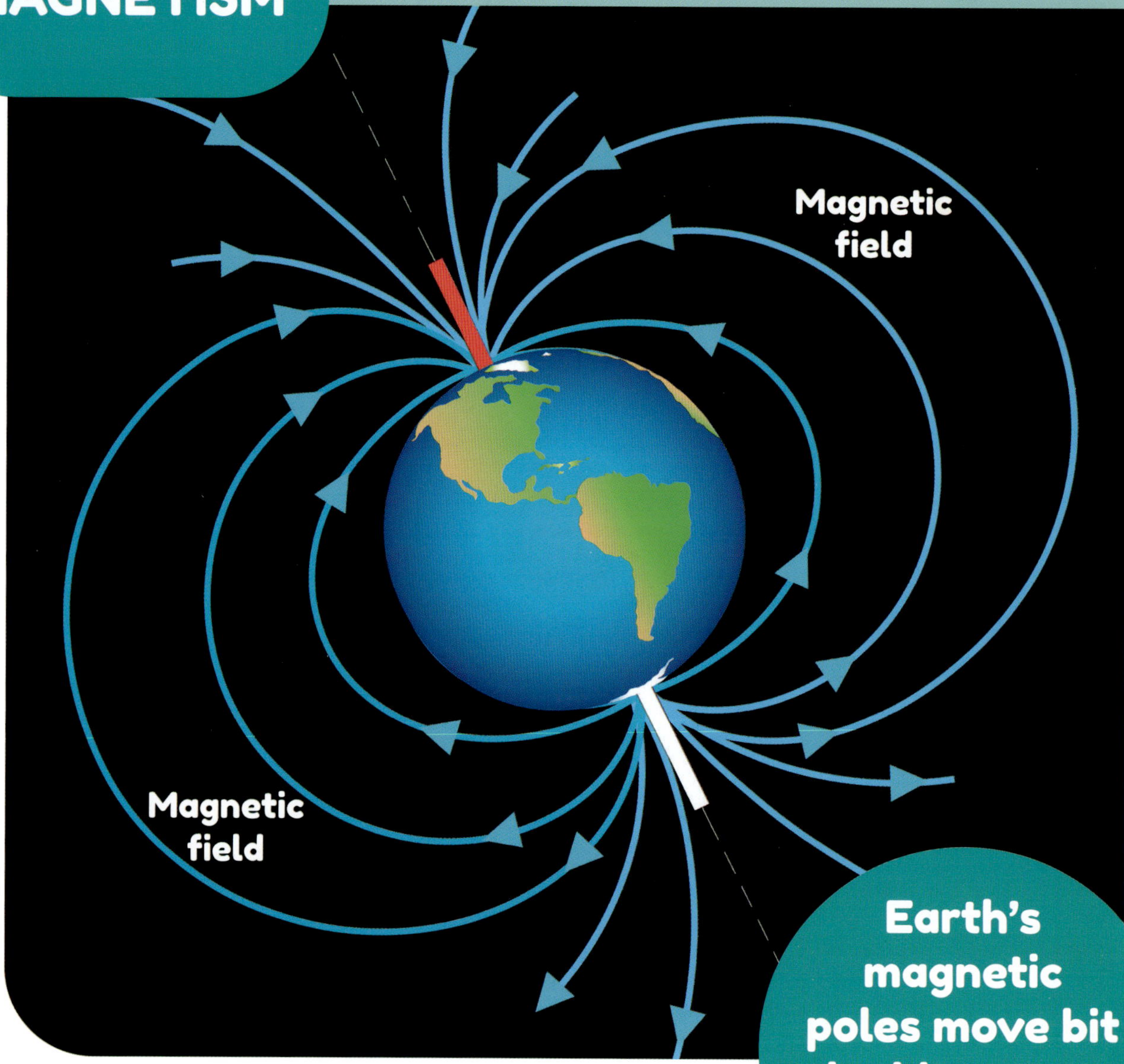

Earth's magnetic poles move bit by bit over a long period of time.

Earth's Poles

Earth has a magnetic north and south pole. These are at the top and bottom of Earth.

Compasses

A compass has a magnet. The north pole of the magnet turns toward Earth's south pole. This is because opposite poles attract. As it does, it moves an arrow to point north.

Auroras

Solar particles bounce off Earth's magnetic field. They make colorful light shows in the night sky called auroras. They appear near Earth's poles.

People use compasses to keep from getting lost outdoors.

GLOSSARY

apply
To put into use, action, or effect.

balanced
Describing two or more things equal in size, amount, or strength.

device
A tool made for a purpose.

mechanical
Relating to physical processes and movement.

observe
To notice or sense something.

physical
Having to do with things that can be experienced through one or more senses.

plane
A flat surface, when describing an inclined plane.

solar
Relating to or made by the Sun.

symbol
Something, such as a letter or a sign, that stands for something else.

vacuum
The absence of matter.

vibrate
To move quickly back and forth.

work
The amount of energy used when something is moved by a force.

TO LEARN MORE

More Books to Read

Barfield, Mike. *Feel the Force: Revealing the Physics Secrets That Rule the Universe*. Laurence King, 2023.

Habibi, Sarah. *Noah's Fascinating World of STEAM Experiments: Chemical Reactions*. Mango, 2023.

Marquardt, Meg. *Space*. Abdo, 2025.

Online Resources

Booklinks
NONFICTION NETWORK
FREE! ONLINE NONFICTION RESOURCES

To learn more about physical science, please visit **abdobooklinks.com** or scan this QR code. These links are routinely monitored and updated to provide the most current information available.

INDEX

PHOTO CREDITS

Cover Photos: Patrick Foto/Shutterstock Images, front (hot air balloon), back; Shutterstock Images, front (ice cream, train)

Interior Photos: Shutterstock Images, 1, 3, 4, 5 (bottom), 6, 7 (top), 8 (left), 9, 12, 16, 17, 18, 20, 23, 26, 30 (top), 31, 34, 37, 38, 42 (bottom), 43, 44, 45 (top), 45 (bottom), 46, 48 (top), 52 (bottom), 53, 54, 56 (top), 56 (bottom), 57 (left), 57 (right), 58, 62, 63, 65, 66, 69, 72 (top), 74, 75, 76, 78 (bottom), 79 (spectrum), 85, 87, 88, 89, 92, 93, 94, 96, 105, 107, 110, 110–111, 113, 116, 118, 119, 120, 121, 123, 124; Nikiteev Konstantin/ Shutterstock Images, 5 (top); Mikhail Grachikov/Shutterstock Images, 7 (bottom), 55 (bottom); Olga Popova/ Shutterstock Images, 8 (right); Science Source, 10; Peter Hermes Furian/Shutterstock Images, 11; Zern Liew/ Shutterstock Images, 13; Jiri Hera/Shutterstock Images, 14; Mara Ze/Shutterstock Images, 15; Uladzimir Zuyeu/Shutterstock Images, 19; Pau Buera/Shutterstock Images, 21; Karen C. Fox/Goddard/SDO/NASA, 22; Sorapop Udomsri/Shutterstock Images, 24, 25; Ezume Images/Shutterstock Images, 27; Ionus Ene/ Shutterstock Images, 28; Zhane Luk/Shutterstock Images, 29; Ben Bryant/Shutterstock Images, 30 (bottom); Amorn Suriyan/Shutterstock Images, 32, 48 (bottom), 115; Steven Salgado/Shutterstock Images, 33; Ground Picture/Shutterstock Images, 35, 50; Wavebreak Media/Shutterstock Images, 36; Vitalii Vitleo/Shutterstock Images, 39; Carolyn Franks/Shutterstock Images, 40; Africa Studio/Shutterstock Images, 41; Sergey Klopotov/ Shutterstock Images, 42 (top); Paul Vinten/Shutterstock Images, 47; Orren Jack Turner/Library of Congress, 49; Mark Garlick/Science Source, 51; Dima Zel/Shutterstock Images, 52 (top); Andy A. Helbling/Shutterstock Images, 55 (top); Red Line Editorial, 59, 61, 117; Craig Lambert Photography/Shutterstock Images, 60; Antonio Guillem/Shutterstock Images, 64; Somchai Som/Shutterstock Images, 67; Virrage Images/Shutterstock Images, 68; Dariusz Jarzabek/Shutterstock Images, 70; iStockphoto, 71, 122; Mila Drumeva/Shutterstock Images, 72 (bottom); Staff Sgt. Sadie Colbert/US Air Force/DVIDS, 73; Agency-Animal-Picture/Getty Images News/Getty Images, 77; NASA, 78 (top); Rufat Bunyadzada/Shutterstock Images, 79 (goggles), 79 (microwave); Noel V. Baebler/Shutterstock Images, 80; Olya Humeniuk/Shutterstock Images, 81; Melissa Phillip/Houston Chronicle/AP Images, 82; Christina Richards/Shutterstock Images, 83; Nikita Rublev/ Shutterstock Images, 84–85; Ljupco Smokovski/Shutterstock Images, 86; Natpant Prommanee/Shutterstock Images, 90; Amparo Garcia/Shutterstock Images, 91; Oleg Kopyov/Shutterstock Images, 95; Ted Kinsman/ Science Source, 98; Westock Productions/Shutterstock Images, 99; GIPhotoStock/Science Source, 100, 101 (top), 101 (bottom); Orion Media Group/Shutterstock Images, 102; Menno van der Haven/Shutterstock Images, 103; Jonathan Weiss/Shutterstock Images, 104; Artur Widak/Anadolu Agency/Getty Images, 106; C. L. Shebley/Shutterstock Images, 108; Tristan Tan/Shutterstock Images, 109; Vasilyev Alexandr/Shutterstock Images, 112; J. J. Gouin/Shutterstock Images, 114; Karbo Kreto/Shutterstock Images, 125 (top); Alexander Chaikin/Shutterstock Images, 125 (bottom)